Helping Hands

In the Ambulance Service

Ruth Thomson

WAYLAND

First published in 2006 by Wayland,
an imprint of Hachette Children's Books

Copyright © Wayland 2006

Editor: Laura Milne
Managing Editor: Victoria Brooker
Senior Design Manager: Rosamund Saunders
Design: Proof Books
Commissioned photography: Chris Fairclough

Additional photography: Thanks are due to the following for
kind permission to reproduce photographs:
pages 18, 19 (top) and 26 London Ambulance Service
page 27 Topfoto

British Library Cataloguing in Publication Data:

Thomson, Ruth
Helping hands in the ambulance service
1. Ambulance service – Juvenile literature
I. Title II. In the ambulance service
362.1'88

ISBN-10: 0-7502-4858-0
ISBN-13: 978-0-7502-4858-7

Printed and bound in China

Hachette Children's Books
A division of Hodder Headline Limited
338 Euston Road, London NW1 3BH

Acknowledgements
The author and publisher would like to thank the following
people for their help and participation in this book:
Pat Andrews, Tom Lynch, Lisa Davies, Nick Goh, David Martin,
Ian Sibthorpe, Robert Fitzgerald, Brian Massey, Tracey
Pidgeon, Ian Bullamore, Steve Jones, Paul Keating, Alex Bass,
Emergency Operations Centre at London Ambulance Service,
Brixton and Oval Ambulance Station, London.

Contents

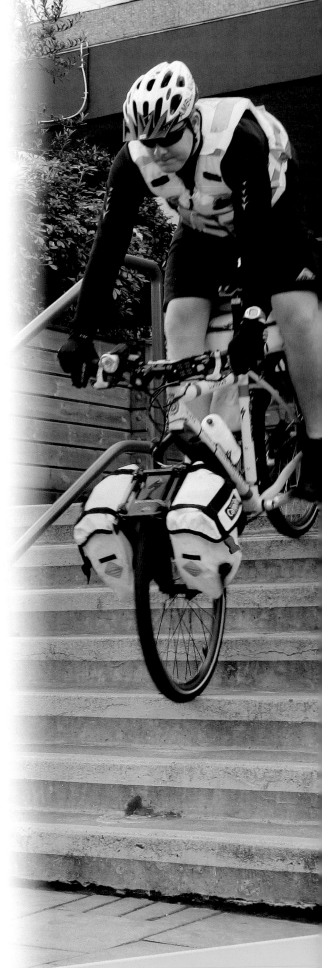

Words in **bold** can be found in the glossary.

The ambulance station

We work for the ambulance service.

We are based at an ambulance station.

Some of us work as ambulance crews.

Some of us are **first responders**.

▼ There are ten ambulance crews at our station. We take turns to work in **shifts**.

There are two people
in each ambulance crew.
One is a **paramedic** and
the other is an emergency
medical **technician**.

We give people
first aid and
take them
to hospital. ▶

▼ I am a first
responder. I work
in a car called a
rapid response unit.

The ambulance

We check the ambulance to make sure it is ready for any **emergency**.

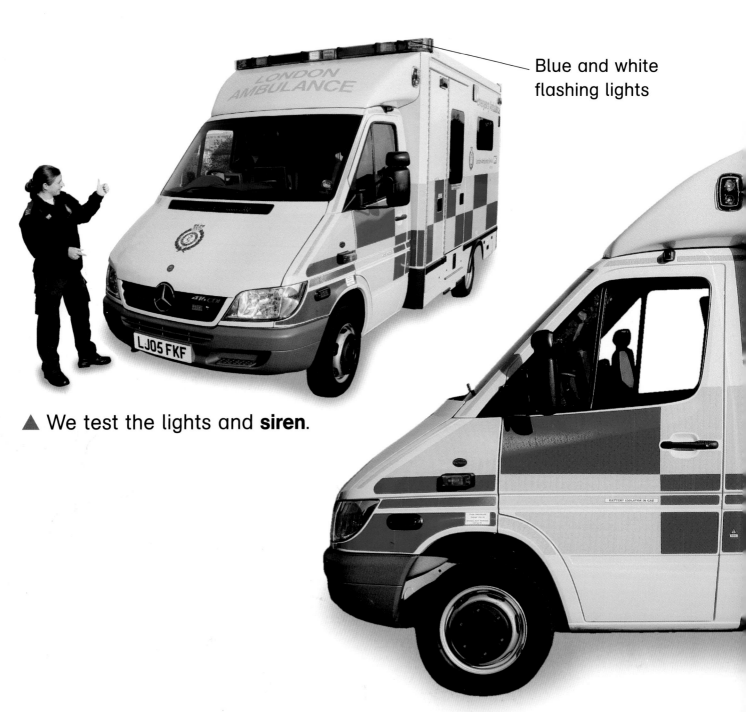

Blue and white flashing lights

▲ We test the lights and **siren**.

We check the tyres, the fuel, the oil and the water. We test the brakes and the windscreen wipers.

▲ The **crest** of the ambulance service

Equipment locker

Door for patients

Spotlight for working at night

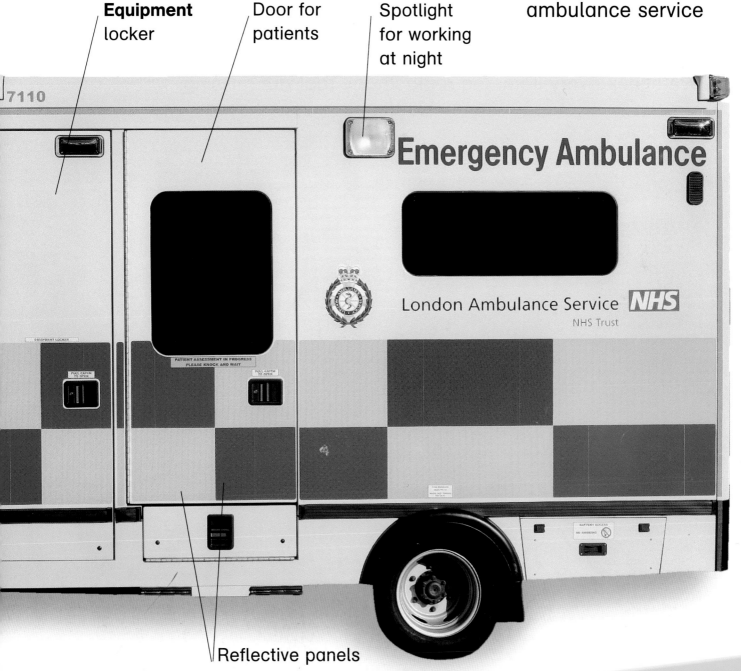

7110

Emergency Ambulance

London Ambulance Service **NHS**
NHS Trust

Reflective panels

Ambulance equipment

An ambulance carries **equipment**
for all sorts of **emergencies**, such as
road accidents, fires, births and falls,
as well as **asthma** or heart attacks.

▼ We check every item and replace any that are missing.

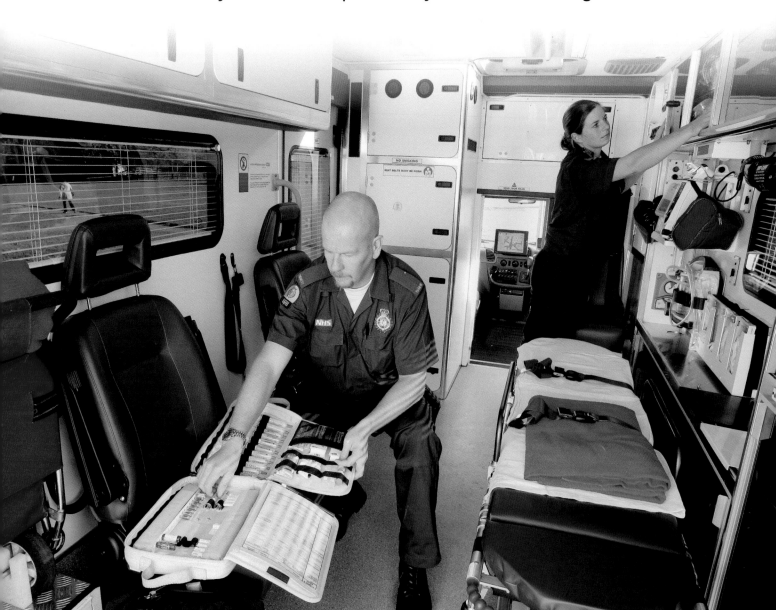

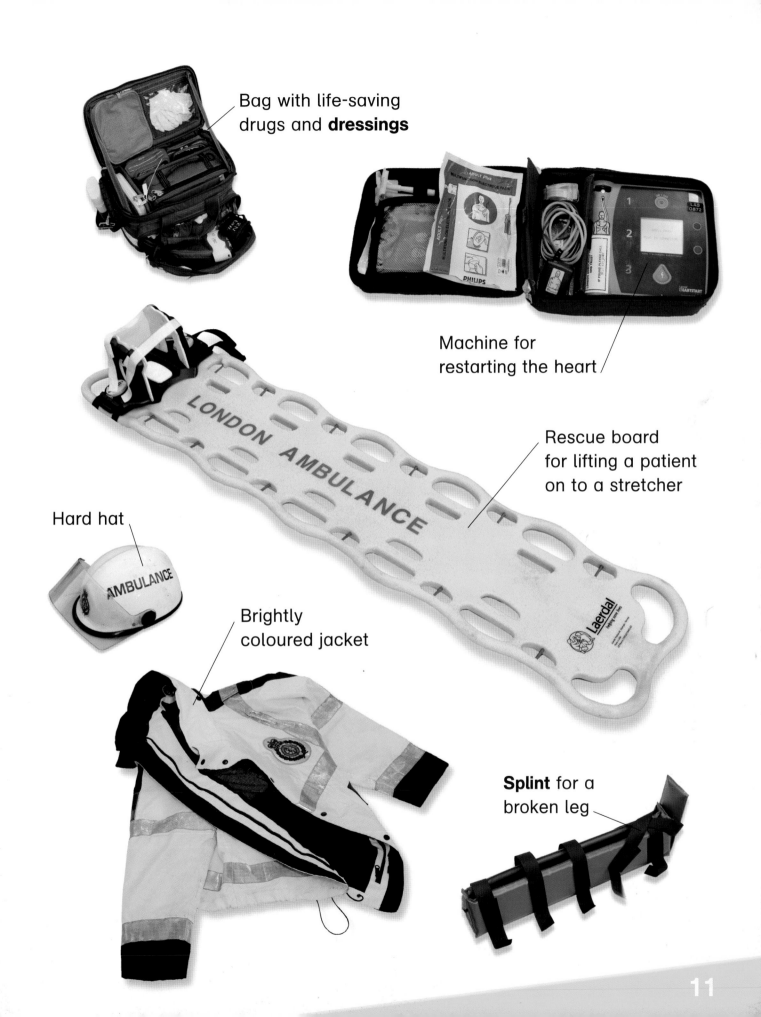

Bag with life-saving drugs and **dressings**

Machine for restarting the heart

Rescue board for lifting a patient on to a stretcher

Hard hat

Brightly coloured jacket

Splint for a broken leg

LONDON AMBULANCE

AMBULANCE

11

First responders

We are called 'first responders' because we help people before an ambulance arrives. We carry life-saving **equipment**. Just by being there quickly we can save a life.

▲ I work on my own. I store all my equipment in my car.

I am a first responder
on a motorbike. ▶

Blue flashing
lights

Powerful
headlights

Panniers
with first aid
equipment

When I'm speeding to an
emergency, people can
easily see me coming.

◀ I put on the **siren**
and all the lights
when I am in a hurry.

Cycle response unit

I am a first responder on a bicycle. I work in the city centre. I can take my bike into shopping centres, shops or even up in a lift.

I make sure I have all my **first aid equipment**. ▶

◀ Each day I test the brakes and lights, and pump up the tyres.

Sometimes I have to cycle down steps. ▶

I wear a T-shirt, shorts and cycling shoes. I also wear a vest with pockets and a belt for my phone, scissors, **latex** gloves, torch and **stethoscope**.

◀ I carry almost everything that an ambulance does.

Map of city centre

Horn

Flashing blue light

Panniers for waterproofs, tool kit and lunch

Drink bottle

Panniers for first aid equipment

Waiting for a call

While the ambulance crew is waiting,
they can relax at the ambulance station.

◀ There is
a roof garden
where we can
sit outside.

We can play pool
while waiting for
a call. ▼

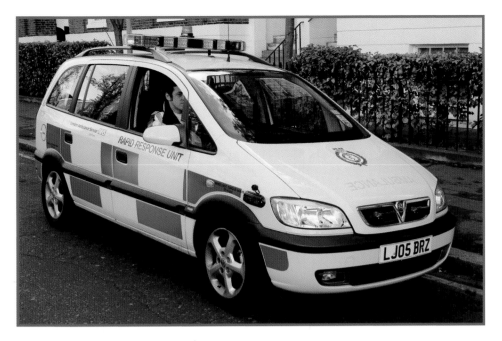

The **first responders** wait at places around town.

◀ I wait at a place called a standby point in a busy area.

▼ When I am out waiting for a call, people often stop to ask me directions.

An emergency call

When people make **emergency** 999 calls, they are put through to the Emergency Operations Centre.

How to call an ambulance

* Dial 999. The call is free.
* Ask for the ambulance service.
* Give the call taker your name and phone number.
* Say the full address of where the emergency is.
* Answer the questions that the call taker asks you.

▼ More than a dozen call takers answer the 999 calls.

Call takers ask where the emergency is and what has happened. They ask questions about the person who needs help, and type the answers on to a computer.

◀ I am a dispatcher. I send out the information about an emergency to the nearest ambulance.

The ambulance receives the message on a screen. ▶

First aid

When a **first responder** arrives at an **emergency**, they treat the patient as quickly as possible.

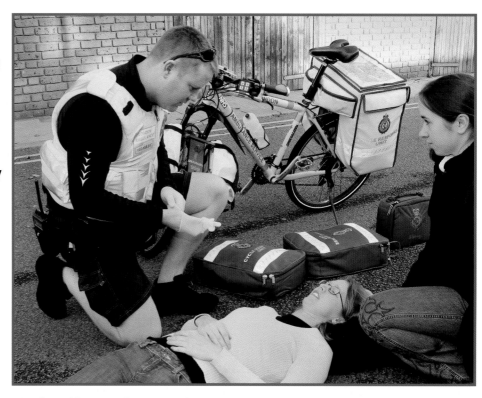

▲ I talk to the patient to see how wide awake she is.

▲ This patient is finding it hard to breathe. I give her some **oxygen**.

▲ I measure her **pulse** and her blood pressure.

I tell the Emergency Operations
Centre on my radio how the patient is,
so that the ambulance crew will know
what to do as soon as they arrive.

The ambulance arrives

When we get an **emergency** call, we drive to the scene as fast and safely as we can. We open the back of the ambulance and collect any **equipment** we need.

We lower down the stretcher from the ambulance. ▶

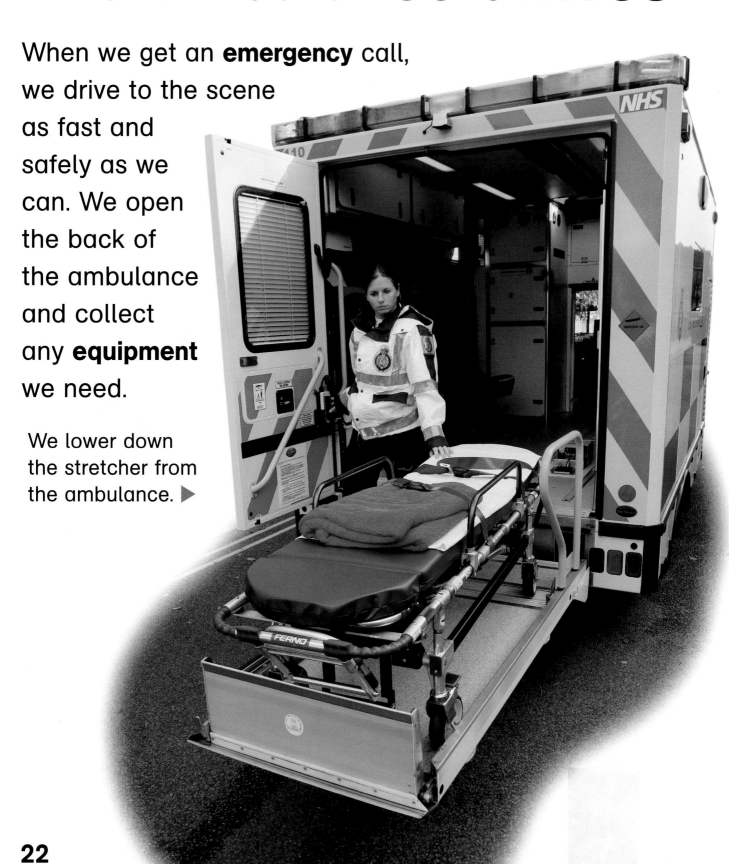

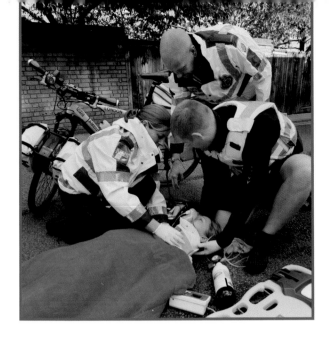

◀ We fix a neck collar around the patient. We cover her with a blanket to keep her warm.

We strap her safely on to the rescue board. ▶

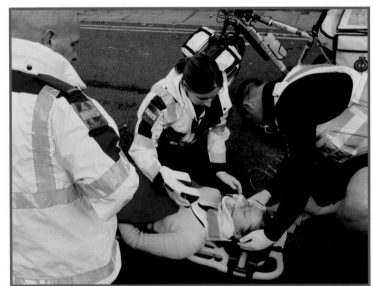

We lift the patient on to the stretcher and wheel her into the ambulance. ▼

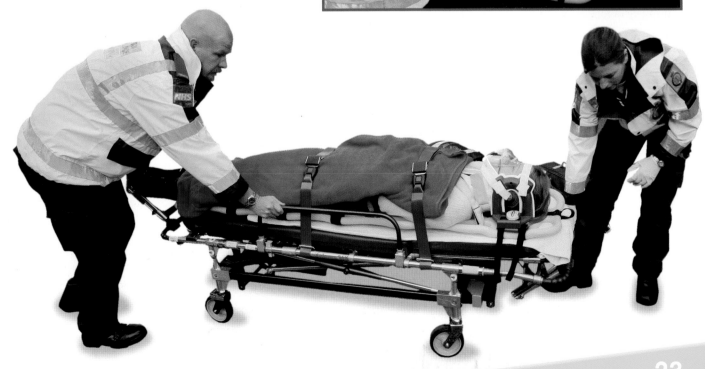

Going to hospital

We speed off to hospital. We turn on the ambulance's **siren** and blue flashing lights. We have to drive through heavy traffic.

▼ Cars quickly move out of our way.

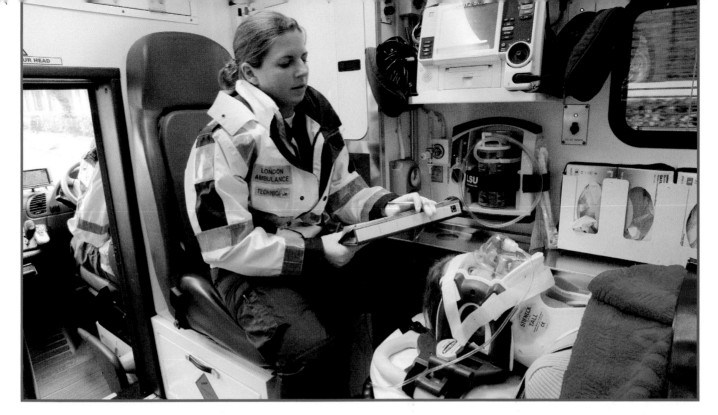

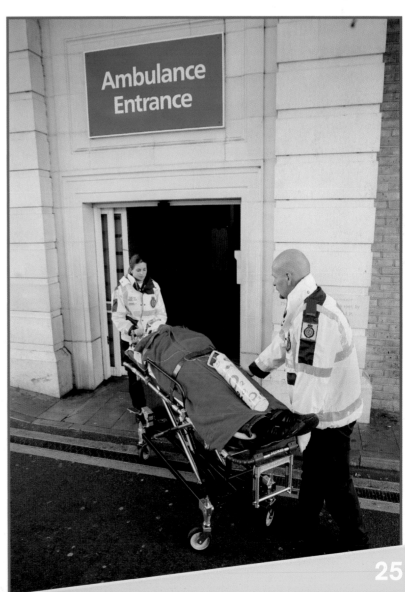

▲ I look after the patient in the back. I watch her breathing. I ask her questions and write down the answers.

We take the patient to the hospital's Accident and Emergency department. Doctors will look after her now. ▶

Teamwork

At some **emergencies**, we team up with the police and firefighters. At a motorway crash, the police stop or control the traffic. Firefighters may have to cut people out of their cars or put out flames.

▲ We give first aid to the injured at a road accident.

If someone is very badly hurt, the air ambulance helicopter is called out. The air ambulance can reach a patient and get them to hospital more quickly than a normal ambulance.

▲ An air ambulance can land almost anywhere.

Glossary

asthma people with asthma sometimes find it hard to breathe

crest the badge or symbol of an organisation such as the ambulance service

dressing a covering, such as a bandage, for a cut or burn

emergency a sudden dangerous event, such as a fire, flood or car crash, which needs instant action

equipment all the things that people use for their job

first aid treatment of a sick or hurt person before a doctor arrives

first responder someone in the ambulance service who arrives to give first aid before an ambulance can get there

latex thin stretchy rubber

oxygen the air that we need to breathe

panniers one of the two storage bags on a motorbike or bicycle

paramedic a highly trained ambulance worker, who can give life-saving drugs

pulse the regular beat that you can feel on your wrist or neck, caused by your heart pumping blood

shift a period of time that a person works

siren a horn that makes a loud noise on ambulances and other emergency vehicles

splint something used to keep a broken leg or arm in the right position

stethoscope an instrument used to listen to the heart and lungs

technician an emergency ambulance worker who helps a paramedic

Quiz

Look back through the book to do this quiz.

1 What telephone number do you dial if you need an ambulance?

2 When does an ambulance use a siren?

3 What is a first responder?

4 When is the air ambulance called out?

5 How many people are there in an ambulance crew? What are they called?

6 When do ambulance workers, police and firefighters team together?

7 What is a rapid response unit?

8 To what part of a hospital does an ambulance take patients?

Answers

1 999.

2 When it is on an emergency call and is in heavy traffic.

3 Someone who helps people before an ambulance arrives.

4 If someone is very badly hurt, in a serious accident.

5 Two people – a paramedic and an emergency medical technician.

6 At a serious emergency, like a motorway crash.

7 A first responder in a car.

8 Accident and Emergency.

Useful contacts

www.sja.org.uk/young_people/badgers.asp

Young people aged 5-10 years old can join the St. John Ambulance as Badgers. They will learn first aid and life-saving skills in a safe and fun environment, as well as making new friends. Visit the website to find a branch near you.

www.londonambulance.nhs.uk

The website of the London Ambulance Service. Look under 'Publications' and read about a character called 'Norman the Ambulanceman'.

It is a job where you know you are doing good and helping people.

Index

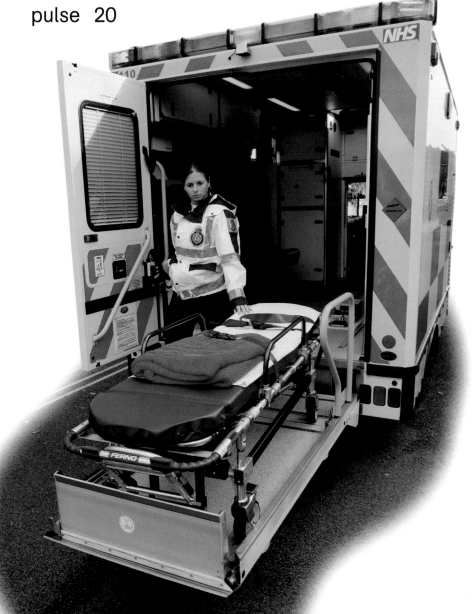